ALASTAIR SCOTT ANDERSON, MA

D1498729

ROMAN MILITARY TOMBSTONES

SHIRE ARCHAEOLOGY

2

Cover photograph
Detail of the tombstone of Sextus Valerius Genialis,
a trooper of the cavalry regiment of Thracians;
Corinium Museum, Cirencester.
(Photograph and copyright author.)

Published by
SHIRE PUBLICATIONS LTD
Cromwell House, Church Street, Princes Risborough,
Aylesbury, Bucks HP17 9AJ, UK.

Series Editor: James Dyer

ISBN 0 85263 571 0

First published 1984

Set in 11 point Times and printed in Great Britain by C. I. Thomas & Sons
(Haverfordwest) Ltd, Press Buildings, Merlins Bridge, Haverfordwest, Dyfed
SA61 1XE.

Contents

4

List of illustrations

Preface

This book has been written for the reader who has an interest in the subject of death and burial in the ancient world; it defines the various types of funerary markers used by the Roman army and explains their context against the background of contemporary views about death and sepulchral procedures. It will be useful to students of Roman Britain who are frustrated by the scarcity of literature available to the non-specialist in this subject, and especially to those whose knowledge of Latin is not great. Tombstones, especially those connected with the Roman army, often inspire great interest among students. This attention is not due to a macabre curiosity about death, but rather to an awareness of the importance of funerary sculpture and inscriptions as primary sources of information about life in the ancient world, the ideas of the living being represented on the tombs of the dead.

Tombstones relate not only to individuals but to society as a whole and this book explains their significance, points out particular areas of interest and removes some of the mystique often associated with their study. Readers should not be deterred by a lack of knowledge of the Latin language. Most Roman inscriptions in Britain, funerary or otherwise, are written in Latin, but the majority are executed in a standard fashion with similar items of information appearing in the same place on each inscription. Details of what to look for and the meanings of the abbreviations most frequently encountered on funerary inscriptions are to be found in chapter 4. The sculptural representations appearing on tombstones are discussed in chapter 5. They reveal many aspects of ancient life in a unique manner, especially with regard to clothing and burial beliefs.

This book deals largely with material dating from the first and second centuries AD, when free-standing tombstones were more common than in the subsequent period. To deal with all funerary art would require greater length than this present study allows and so it concerns itself almost exclusively with military tombstones, as they form a succinct and particularly interesting group. In order to make the material included more comprehensive tombstones from the Roman provinces of Germany and Pannonia have been illustrated but most of the examples used are from Britain, which has much excellent material.

It gives me great pleasure to thank the following people for their assistance in connection with this book: Professor J. J. Wilkes, Institute of Archaeology, London, for supplying me with both information and ideas; Professor J. S. Wacher, Leicester University, for helpful advice; Dr A. K. B. Evans, Leicester University, who gave me considerable help with the final draft of this study; the numerous museum staff who assisted me with information and illustrations; and Professor D. B. Saddington, University of Zimbabwe, whose work on the dating of Roman military tombstones awakened my own interest in the subject.

TABLE OF ROMAN EMPERORS AND THEIR DYNASTIES

Date AD	Emperor	Periods to which reference is made in the text	
-14	Augustus	Augustan	
14-37	Tiberius	Tiberian	Julio-Claudian
37-41	Caligula (Gaius)		or
41-54	Claudius	Claudian	Pre-Flavian
54-68	Nero	Neronian	
69-79	Vespasian	Vespasianic	
79-81	Titus		Flavian
81-96	Domitian	Domitianic	
98-117	Trajan	Trajanic	
117-138	Hadrian	Hadrianic	
138-161	Antoninus Pius		
161-180	Marcus Aurelius		Antonine
180-192	Commodus		

1
The Roman army

There are more than 450 Roman tombstones known from Britain. Some of them commemorate civilians, but many, including the finest examples, relate either to serving soldiers or to veterans and their families. Much of what is known about the Roman army has resulted from the study of tombstones and, conversely, an understanding of army organisation is useful if funerary monuments are to be fully appreciated. The majority of relief-decorated free-standing Roman tombstones found in Britain date to the first and second centuries AD and many originally marked graves containing cremations. They frequently display delicately worked floral patterns and representations of mythological creatures and they often commemorate the deceased not only in words but also in sculpted figure scenes.

At the centre of the Empire, during the reigns of Trajan and Hadrian, inhumation replaced cremation as the most popular method for the disposal of the dead and it became the fashion for those who were wealthy enough to bury the dead within lavishly carved marble sarcophagi or decorated lead coffins. The trend evident in Italy for this more elaborate form of burial gained acceptance more slowly in the peripheral provinces of the Empire. In Britain the practice of cremation and its accompanying use of free-standing tombstones retained its popularity for much longer than in Mediterranean areas. However, even in Britain, some stones which appear to have been free-standing may have formed parts of larger funerary structures such as mausolea, although this is perhaps less likely in the case of serving soldiers of the lower ranks.

In the early Empire the Roman army was divided into three basic elements : the Praetorian Guard, the Legions, and the Auxilia. The Praetorian Guard was the élite of the army and its members were normally stationed in Rome. As imperial bodyguards they were responsible for the safety of the Emperor, and when he left Rome to lead his troops on campaign they accompanied him. In AD 43 Claudius brought the Praetorians with him when he visited Britain during his campaign of conquest. Of more importance in the frontier provinces were the legions. They were the backbone of the Roman army, well trained and heavily armed infantry regiments composed entirely of Roman citizens. There were usually between twenty-five and thirty legions stationed in the frontier areas. Britain normally maintained a garrison of three legions, but for long periods in the first century there were four.

The total establishment of the legion was about six thousand men. Each legion was commanded by a *legatus legionis,* a senator, usually in his thirties. Below the *legatus* were six military tribunes and a *praefectus castrorum,* who was responsible for the organisation of the camp, training and equipment: unlike the other senior officers, whose terms of service lasted only for two or three years, he was a professional soldier who had spent many years in the army, having formerly been the chief centurion of a legion. Ranking below these officers were the sixty centurions of the legion, the men directly responsible for the centuries which they commanded. One of the finest tombstones from Britain is of a centurion, Marcus Favonius Facilis (plate 1), who served in the Twentieth Legion and died at Colchester in the years shortly after the conquest.

The centurions were the men who kept the legion running from day to day, but, even more, they were professional soldiers, usually with many years experience, who provided the continuity so necessary to the efficiency of an organisation in which the senior officers' commands were of such short duration. Each century numbered eighty men and included an *optio,* the centurion's second in command; a *signifer,* a standard bearer, who was also treasurer of the soldiers' savings and burial club funds; and a *tesserarius,* who received the daily watchword and dealt with guard duties. In addition, there were a number of *immunes,* soldiers whose specialist duties exempted them from fatigues. Some of these, such as the *librarii caducorum,* who dealt with the wills and properties of those killed on active service, were attached to the legionary headquarters staff.

Other notable members of the legionary establishment were the *aquilifer* (plate 5), who carried the eagle standard *(aquila),* the sacred symbol of each legion, and the *imaginifer,* who carried a standard bearing the image of the emperor (plates 6-7). Men such as these standard bearers could, in time, become centurions; and one, Petronius Fortunatus, who started his military career in *I Italica* in Lower Moesia (see fig. 1), after serving as an *optio* and *signifer* saw service as a centurion in twelve other legions. For the *miles gregarius,* the common soldier, opportunities were less frequent and many served their time without promotion. Even so, numerous tombstones record the memory of these lower ranks, often in considerable style.

The third basic component of the early imperial military system, the auxilia, was split into three types of unit, cavalry, infantry and part-mounted regiments, each numbering either five hundred or one thousand men. Such forces had originally been composed of native allies led by their own chieftains but had been regularised and integrated into the army by Augustus at the beginning of the imperial period. Cavalry units, commanded by a *praefectus*, were called *alae* (wings) and within each regiment were divided up into *turmae*, troops of thirty-two men led by a *decurio*. Infantry units, *cohortes*, were divided into centuries, eighty men strong, as in the legions. Less is known about the part-mounted type of unit, the *cohors equitata*, but each appears to have consisted of 380 infantry and 120 cavalry. Most of the men serving in the auxilia lacked Roman citizenship, but many, in keeping with their legionary counterparts, still aspired to lavish funerary monuments, leaving inscribed on their tombstones a wealth of information relating to their names, origins, rank and regiments.

2
Roman funerary practices

The Romans were preoccupied with death and burial customs in a manner rarely seen in modern civilisations. This may be explained in part by the relatively short lifespan experienced in many ancient societies, especially among the lower classes, in a world where disease, poor diet and physical labour often brought about death before the age of forty. However, more relevant to Roman society were the beliefs engendered by ancestor worship and the cult of the dead, which gave men a distinct spiritual link with their deceased forebears. Although the Romans entertained many different theories concerning death and the afterlife, prevalent was the belief that a dead man continued to exist as an independent entity in the tomb. It was thought that in this afterlife the dead could still influence events among the living, sometimes reappearing for example in dreams, and that they were subject to the same needs as the living, obliged to eat and drink, and reliant upon those alive to provide for these necessities. The dead were considered to be especially likely to feel resentment if their passing had not been duly celebrated or if their needs in the grave were neglected, and so death was followed by an outburst of grief on the part of the living relatives, continued by prolonged manifestations of mourning to prove to the deceased that he was truly lamented. The tomb was to be an eternal house and objects used in life were placed in the grave to provide comfort for the dead — toys for children, toilet articles for women, tools or weapons for men. In the Roman world a man drew much of his status in society from the position and achievements of his ancestors; in marking their passing, it was very unwise not to show the dead the greatest respect.

Much less is known about death and burial in the Roman army than about the customs and beliefs in civilian life. Soldiers killed in battle were collectively cremated, but the elaborate funerary monuments erected to soldiers who died in the normal course of service and who left instructions for the setting up of tombstones in their wills illustrate that they were no less concerned with their public images in the afterlife than were their civilian counterparts. Indeed, the philosophy behind the military and the civilian funeral can have differed but little.

Inhumation rather than cremation was the primitive burial rite in Rome, but the two soon came to be practised side by side and from *c* 400 BC onwards cremation was the normal method for the disposal of the dead. It continued to be so until the second century AD, when in most areas of the Empire inhumation once again became popular. After death, it was customary for the body to be washed and anointed and finally dressed ready for a period of lying in state. The funeral that followed began with a procession in which the deceased, lying on a funerary couch, was carried on a bier to the place of burial. In civilian life the bearers were male relatives, friends or the man's newly liberated slaves; in the army, this duty would have been performed by fellow soldiers. At the front of the procession musicians, pipers, trumpeters or horn-blowers heralded the approach of the bier while at the rear of the cortège relatives and friends showed their respect.

The earliest of Roman laws, the *Twelve Tables,* forbade burial or cremation within the city. This regulation was later translated into municipal law in Rome's colonies and accordingly burials normally took place outside towns, in areas not used for agriculture, often along the main roads beyond the city limits. Roman military establishments were apparently not exempt from such regulations relating to the disposal of the dead, and soldiers' tombs are usually located well beyond the fort perimeter, again at the roadside. The discovery of the tombstones of Marcus Favonius Facilis and Longinus (plates 1 and 15) to the south-west of Colchester, only a short distance apart, indicates the presence of such an early cemetery outside the legionary fortress which preceded the later city.

When the funeral procession arrived at the place of interment the burial rites were performed. The corpse and the couch on which it lay were lifted on to a rectangular wooden funerary pyre and the body was burnt. After the cremation the ashes and burnt bones of the body were collected together and poured into a receptacle for burial. These ash containers were sometimes made from marble, silver or bronze, but more common were glass vessels and pottery jars.

After the funeral a banquet took place at the grave. This feast, the *silicernium,* in honour of the dead, was followed by another, the *cena novendialis,* eaten on the ninth day after the funeral. At these banquets it was considered that the spirits of the dead were somehow able to join their living relatives to enjoy the food and drink provided. Sometimes offerings of food were left on the grave; other graves were equipped with a pipe, from the burial up to the ground surface, down which offerings could be poured to fulfil the supposed material needs of the dead. In the army these customs were presumably maintained by the dead man's colleagues or by his concubine, as serving soldiers did not possess the right of marriage.

In the first century AD a large number of centurions, both legionary and auxiliary, and many legionaries were of Italian origin, and military funerals are likely to have reflected contemporary civilian practices at Rome. To these men, the importance of remembrance by the living was paramount; and since the heir of the dead man gained in status through the good works of his benefactor, lavish funeral orations were delivered and magnificent tombstones erected to ensure the memory of the deceased. This was a manifestation of the concept of *memoria,* a belief that all the values for which the dead stood lived on in their descendants; it was an indefinable power which linked family members, real or adopted, from generation to generation. That funerals remained rather grandiose, even in the army, is suggested by the magnificence of many of the tombstones discovered on military sites, recording not only citizens of Italian origin but also non-citizens serving in the auxilia.

The adoption of Mediterranean-style stelae by auxiliaries, many of them from frontier areas, illustrates not only the civilising influence of Rome but also the dissemination of the Latin language. Some of the auxiliary cavalry tombstones found in Britain and Germany, belonging to ordinary troopers, are among the finest examples of provincial funerary art in the Empire and the inscriptions found on them, designed to impress and undoubtedly appreciated even by the common soldier, suggest that even the lowest ranks in many regiments understood some Latin, despite their barbarian backgrounds. Indeed, the presence or absence of classical-style tombstones can sometimes reveal the differing progress of Romanisation among auxiliary units. For example, there is an absence of early inscriptions relating to Batavian units from the Low Countries and this, together with a revolt against Rome in AD 69 by Batavian regiments serving in the Rhineland, suggests that Romanisation among the auxilia from this area was a slow process.

When a soldier died, the cost of his funeral was paid for by the regimental burial club into which every man paid compulsory fees, along with other deductions from his pay for rations, boots and clothing. The burial club fund was administered by the regimental standard bearers and ensured each soldier a decent burial. The annual contribution to the fund comprised a relatively small proportion of each man's pay but the burial grant allowed on death was probably fixed at a standard rate rather than being directly related to the accumulated payments of each individual. This was the practice in civilian burial associations and in a number of cases, in North Africa and Italy, where the expenditure on a tomb is recorded, a standard cost related to burial-club outlay is suggested. However, as can be observed in any large museum collection, Roman tombstones show surprising differences in both scale and design. These variations are sometimes due to the quality of workmanship or the availability of sculptors but cost is frequently a governing factor and expenditure differs seemingly inexplicably between persons of the same rank or status. Some individuals undoubtedly cared more for their reputation among the living than others and were prepared to pay large sums of money to ensure the provision of a fine tomb; others seem to have spent nothing extra, relying on the insurance provided by the regimental burial fund. Status and wealth are reflected in tomb expenditure with, in general, those at the top levels of society paying more, but there are exceptions. Strong individual piety might result in a common soldier paying almost as much for his tomb as a less religious, or perhaps less cautious, centurion, despite an enormous difference in pay levels between the two. Occasionally, a soldier would spend more than a year's pay on his tomb, although usually the amount was much less.

Under Roman law the family was the legal unit recognised by the state and within it the head of the family *(paterfamilias)* was the sole fully legal person able not only to own property but also to dispose of it. Any possessions acquired by a son were automatically owned by his father and were his to dispose of. In a system where young men were expected to volunteer for military service and be stationed on the distant frontiers of the Empire, far from home and family, this lack of legal status for all but the *paterfamilias* was clearly undesirable. Roman soldiers were both well looked after and well paid by contemporary standards and much of their money went into a personal savings account managed by the army but a man could not be expected to serve loyally if his rewards were not his to control. Consequently, from the time of Augustus soldiers were given rights over the property which they acquired during the course of service. This is reflected in inscriptions on many tombstones which mention heirs and their part in the erection of the monument, often in accordance with the dead man's will. If a man had a son, by his concubine, then he would usually be the deceased's heir. Failing this, a brother

serving in the same regiment or stationed nearby might be
mentioned as an heir. If a man had no blood relatives, an heir
could be adopted who would take the family name of his patron
and preserve its memory. In this way, a soldier would pass on his
possessions after death and also his instructions for his well-being
in the tomb.

It was the responsibility of a man's heirs to make the funeral
arrangements, although in the Roman world there were professional undertakers to whom they could turn. Roman wills often
contained detailed instructions as to how the deceased's tomb was
to be constructed and maintained and undoubtedly this is one of
the main reasons for the variety of designs of sepulchral
monuments to be found. In order not to displease the dead, the
instructions would have been carried out to the letter; if an heir
did not accept his obligations, according to the will, a second-
named heir could always inherit in his place. By such devices
provision for the afterlife was assured, at least for a time.

3
Tombstone classification

The free-standing tombstone or stele of the Roman world evolved from established classical Greek designs, in particular deriving from temple architecture employing triangular pediments and supporting columns. However, on many tombstones the predilection with horizontal and vertical elements, so markedly Greek in concept, is replaced by the more plastic lines of Roman style, notably in the use of the arch. In consequence of this ancestry certain parts of tombstones have come to be described in architectural terms and these are shown in fig. 3.

The origins of the stele decorated with carved figures can be traced back to Greek prototypes dating to the fourth to sixth centuries BC, but Roman examples descend directly from later Hellenistic types. Although owing much to the architectural style of buildings, Italian provincial stelae are perhaps more closely related to the design of the household *aedicula* or family shrine. This often consisted of a niche containing a statue and surmounted by a pediment supported on small columns, a construction reflecting grand architecture on a domestic scale. An additional influence may be seen in the portrait busts of deceased ancestors, a feature of Roman funeral display, which were sometimes kept in cupboards in the family household. From representations on figured stelae it is known that these small cupboards could be surmounted by a pitched roof. Gabled tombstones displaying a carved portrait bust may therefore owe their design ultimately to these small cabinets.

The differences in the design of tombstones, especially those relating to the army, are both interesting and significant, in chronological, artistic, social and economic terms. Certain types display features which are peculiar to a restricted geographical area or a particular craftsman while other forms appear to be ubiquitous. In order to identify these variations a number of classifications may be suggested referring to criteria as different as epigraphic content and architectural aspects. Identifications based on the latter, such as on the presence or absence of an architrave at the base of a pediment (see fig. 3) or the inclusion of a conch-shell ornament at the top of a niche (see plate 5), can be very informative about techniques used by individual regional workshops but tend to be of less interest to the more general student of tombstones. Accordingly, a classification based on overall appearance and information content has been adopted here. Four main types of Roman military tombstones are found in Britain.

1. Inscription and simple decoration (figs. 4, 5, 6)

Tombstones bearing only inscriptions are among the earliest and most widespread of funerary monuments in the Roman world. In Britain most tombstones display some form of decoration, however rudimentary, either in the form of a simple moulding around the edge of the inscribed panel or basic plant motifs such as floral rosettes. They may have flat, round or gabled tops and the inscription may be enclosed within a rectangular, gabled or arched panel. Both plain and decorated pediments are common. From the time of Augustus tombstones of this simple design are found bearing epitaphs relating to ordinary Roman soldiers. Those with more intricate floral patterns were particularly popular in the Julio-Claudian and Flavian periods but the type continued into the second century and beyond. They are found in many areas of the Empire, often with little variation in appearance, as can be observed by comparing fig. 5, from Wroxeter, and plate 9, from Carnuntum in the Danube province of Pannonia. In addition to the more complex designs mentioned above, isolated or sometimes grouped individual motifs are frequently found on these stelae; rosettes are particularly common, for example on fig. 6, from Lincoln, and plate 10, another stone from Carnuntum, two representations where although there is a minor difference in detail the concept is identical.

2. Standing figures (plates 1-3 and 5-8)

Tombstones portraying one or more standing figures in relief are relatively numerous amongst British finds. They were common throughout the first and second centuries and can be paralleled in all the northern and western provinces of the Empire. Although examples frequently show only a single figure, family groups can be included, such as on the tombstone erected at York, during his lifetime, by Gaius Aeresius Saenus, veteran of *Legio VI Victrix,* to commemorate his deceased wife and two children as well as himself. The earliest tombstone from Britain belonging to this category, and also the best artistically, is that of Marcus Favonius Facilis (plate 1), centurion of *Legio XX,* discovered in 1868 at Colchester, in a cemetery to the south-west of the early legionary fortress and subsequent *colonia.* As he is not described as a veteran on his epitaph, Facilis was presumably a serving centurion in the fortress garrison before AD 49, when the site was turned over for use as a colony for retired legionaries. This stone probably owes its fine state of preservation to being thrown face down by rebels at the time of the revolt of Boudica in AD 60. As a sculpture, the carved relief of Facilis displays many of the characteristics of good quality first-century workmanship and will have been produced by a legionary craftsman well versed in classical tradition. Later funerary reliefs attempted by native artisans were rarely as aesthetically successful. In general, however, the full-figure style was effective in the depiction of deceased soldiers, especially standard bearers, where height was essential if an *aquila* (plate 5) or *signum* (plate 8) was to be represented in full.

A subdivision of this category, found on early tombstones on the continent, comprises stones where the deceased is shown only from the waist up. Perhaps the best known of all Roman military tombstones is of this type, although it is unlikely to be a true grave marker, but rather a cenotaph in commemoration of Marcus Caelius, a legionary centurion who died in the Varian disaster of AD 9 (plate 2). In this catastrophe, an ambush in thick forest far beyond the Rhine, German tribesmen annihilated three Roman legions, and their commander, Quintilius Varus, took his own life. As it was not until six years later that a force under the Roman general Germanicus visited the site of the battle, to bury the dead, it is very unlikely that the deceased was actually buried beneath the Caelius monument. A further fine example of this style is the early first-century tombstone of Gaius Largennius (fig. 3), of *Legio II Augusta*, which was later to take part in the invasion of Britain. This stone, from Strasbourg, portrays Largennius almost as if he is leaning out of a window, with his military apron hanging forward over the sill and in front of the inscribed panel.

3. Rider reliefs (plates 14-24)

Of great importance for the study of *alae* is the series of tombstones bearing a relief of a mounted cavalryman in action. Such stelae are uniquely military in character and have no known Roman or Italian funerary prototypes. Indeed, the main concentrations of these stones are in the Rhineland and Britain, both areas where auxiliary units were stationed close to legionary bases where craftsmen of the standard required for the production of the finer cavalry stelae were available. The type is essentially, though not exclusively, first-century in date. The earliest examples are found in Germany from the middle years of the reign of Tiberius to the principate of Claudius and are frequently associated with Gallic units such as the *ala Longiniana, Pomponiana* or *Indiana,* which formed the élite of Roman cavalry regiments. These stones usually portray a leaping horse and rider, worked in high relief, in either a niche or recessed panel (plate 14). The type is simple in concept yet can often be executed with conspicuous regard to detail. From this prototype developed two other forms, the mounted cavalryman riding down a barbarian foe, who is usually lying prostrate between the horse's hooves (plate 15-19), and a further variety showing the same scene but with the addition of a servant in the background (plates 20-1). It is the former of these two styles that is found in Britain.

Many of the troops who invaded Britain in AD 43 had previously been stationed in Germany and they brought with them many traditions current in the Rhineland at that time. Several examples of funerary art found in Britain owe much to the styles and techniques of the Rhineland workshops, and perhaps none more than cavalry tombstones with rider reliefs. Britain has produced a number of relatively well preserved figured cavalry stelae, seven of which are illustrated. The design of all seven is based on the theme of the victorious cavalryman riding down the vanquished foe, and differences between them are in detail rather than conception. All are first-century in date, the earliest being that of Longinus from Colchester (plate 15), and the latest the stele of Flavinus from Corbridge (plate 17). Of the seven, two do not belong to *alae*, Rufus Sita (plate 24) and Tiberius Claudius Tirintius (plate 23) having been riders in *cohortes equitatae*, while two others, Sextus Valerius Genialis (plate 16) and Flavinus, were standard bearers. Four of these stones relate to Thracian regiments.

These rider reliefs undoubtedly constitute the most animated and uniform series of funerary monuments in the north-western provinces, yet the ancestry of this group is in some doubt. As mentioned above, there are no Italian prototypes and the most frequently quoted forerunner of the series is the Greek stele of Dexileos, in Athens, datable to 394 BC. This stone, which depicts a horseman riding down a cowering foe, seems too early in date to have influenced the first-century AD Rhineland series. But a tombstone from Abdera in southern Thrace, of the first century

BC, portraying a horseman and his servant (similar to Rhineland examples, plates 20-1), although omitting a prostrate foe, offers a more plausible parallel. It may be no coincidence that the 'rider stele' made its appearance at a time when auxiliary units from Thrace were first transferred to the Rhine area. One of the most important deities in Thrace was a rider-god and the connection between man and horse was a fundamental tenet of Thracian society. A number of these 'rider stelae' commemorate Thracians or men in regiments of Thracian origin and presumably tradition and they may illustrate religious and social connections more specific than has been previously envisaged. Whatever their origin, tombstones of this type were obviously popular in the first century, being assimilated into the funerary procedures of various regiments, the diffusion of the style being due to its design, which enshrined for the individual the ethos of the Roman cavalryman.

4. Funerary banquet (plate 12)

Another type of tombstone found in Britain and Germany is that depicting a funerary banquet. The type shows the deceased, dressed usually in civilian costume, facing forward and supported by the left elbow, reclining on a couch, in front of which stands a low three-legged table. The design can be traced back to Roman and Etruscan sepulchral tradition but the British examples derive directly from Rhineland models, although they fail to attain the high standards of workmanship displayed on the German examples. The figure scene represents either a funerary meal consumed at the tomb, in which the dead person's soul was believed to take part, or a banquet for the departed in the other world. A number of tombstones of this design have been found at Chester, although several are purely civilian in character. Two further sepulchral stones showing the funerary banquet have been discovered in a cemetery at Shirva, east of Auchendavy, on the Antonine Wall in Scotland.

4
Tombstone inscriptions

Latin and Greek inscriptions from the Roman period are the most important single source of material for the study of the history and administration of the Empire. They are contemporary documents unaffected by the mistakes and alterations of later copyists and present the modern scholar with an immense reservoir of information. In the first and second centuries most were cut in monumental capital letters, the work being done by craftsmen of great skill, whose lettering was not merely well executed but also competently placed with an eye to the overall composition of the inscription. Later work can be rather crude, with an increasing frequency of combined letters (ligatures) from the second century onwards. In Latin inscriptions, usually, the use of conventional components is prominent, particularly abbreviations, which are frequently made by leaving letters off at the ends of words. Some are standard, such as *HSE (hic situs est,* 'here he lies'), but others are truncated to suit the taste of the individual or the amount of space available on the stone. This feature and the further complication that words do not always terminate at the end of a line but may run on to the next can cause some confusion for the novice epigrapher. Fortunately, individual words, and sometimes separate letters, are frequently followed by a stop. In good work a triangle or a leaf is used; in poor work a dot is usual. This is normally central to the letters and not placed at their foot as is the modern full stop.

Tombstones provide one of the main sources of epigraphic evidence and more than 450 are known from Roman Britain. Among these funerary inscriptions several merchants are represented, not a surprising occurrence in a frontier province; many commemorate soldiers or their wives, but the size of the civilian population is, in general, poorly reflected. On these sepulchral monuments inscriptions tend to have a similar format and use standard basic abbreviations for the more commonly occurring funerary formulae. Because of the very elaborate naming system used by male Roman citizens for formal purposes, on many inscriptions not only can the name of the deceased be ascertained but also that of his father, the name of the voting tribe to which the dead man belonged, and his place of origin or domicile. Additionally, on military tombstones, information concerning the deceased's regiment, length of service and rank is usually included as well as his age at death.

During the Empire the formal name and description of a male citizen consisted of six elements. First came the *praenomen* or forename, usually abbreviated to the first letter only but occasionally to more, such as A (Aulus), C (Gaius), CN (Gnaeus), L (Lucius), M (Marcus), P (Publius), Q (Quintus), SEX (Sextus), S or SP (Spurius), TI or TIB (Tiberius), and T (Titus). The *praenomen* was a personal name, given in infancy but probably not officially recognised until manhood was achieved.

Next came the *nomen gentilicium,* a family or clan name equivalent to the modern surname. The *nomen* usually ends in -ius, as in Aelius, Flavius, Julius and Ulpius, but rare forms may end with -anus or -enus, for example, the *nomen* Alfenus. Following this was the filiation or patronymic, consisting of the father's *praenomen* and the word *filius,* meaning son. Next appeared the name of the voting tribe to which the deceased belonged, also usually abbreviated, as in COR (Cornelia), GAL (Galeria), POI (Pollia) or VOL (Voltinia). The tribe or 'voting district' was an essential part of a Roman citizen's name. There were thirty-five tribes forming voting units and which also comprised the basis for the census, army recruitment and tax collection. Assignment to a particular tribe was determined by the location of property holdings or place of residence. Originally a tribe would be based in one place but as Roman hegemony expanded many tribes came to be made up of several separated districts.

The fifth element was the third part of the citizen's personal name, the *cognomen,* originally an unofficial name or nickname. The *cognomen* appears much later than the *praenomen* or *nomen,* but as early as 44 BC by the *lex Iulia municipalis,* legislation relating to municipal administration inscribed on a bronze tablet found at Heraclea in southern Italy, officials concerned with taking a census were required to register *cognomina* as well as the other names. Some *cognomina* derived from personal peculiarities but others were honorific, perhaps recalling personal military achievements in other countries, such as Africanus, Hispanus or Macedonicus. The final element of the formal description recorded a man's place of origin, *origo,* or domicile, *domus.*

The combination of the three personal names *(praenomen, nomen* and *cognomen)* is known as the *tria nomina* and was the mark of the Roman citizen. Originally the first two components sufficed for purposes of identification, but the choice of *praenomina* was severely limited and there must have been hundreds of men bearing a name such as Servius Sulpicius or Marcus Porcius. Consequently, to differentiate between these men, a third name, the *cognomen,* was necessary so that Marcus Porcius Cato could be distinguished from other Marci Porcii. Usually the eldest son of a family received the same *praenomen* and *cognomen* as his father, while the second son, although often bearing the same *praenomen,* frequently derived his cognomen from his mother's name. For example, the eldest son of Titus Flavius Vespasianus (the emperor Vespasian) and Flavia Domitilla was named Titus Flavius Vespasianus (the emperor Titus), and the second son Titus Flavius Domitianus (the emperor Domitian). By the time of the invasion of Britain in AD 43 it was normal for Roman citizens to bear the *tria nomina* but it was not quite universal and the first governor of Britain, Aulus Plautius, was an exception, having only two names. With the advent of the Empire the tribal function, so vital for electoral purposes in the Republic, became less important in practice but continued in formal usage. However, as the Empire expanded it became more necessary to list a man's *origo* as more citizens lived at places other than Rome.

On military tombstones the soldier's name is usually followed by his rank, for example *miles* (soldier), *centurio* (centurion), *eques* (horseman or cavalry trooper) or *duplicarius* (an NCO receiving twice the pay of a trooper). Next appears the name of his regiment, such as *ala I Thracum,* a cavalry regiment, followed by his age at death, as in *annorum XXV* (aged twenty-five), and his length of service expressed in the number of annual remunerations received as *stipendiorum XXII* (of twenty-two years' service), or more rarely, *aerorum XV* (of fifteen years' service).

The inscription may end with a reference to the man's heirs, who caused the tombstone to be erected, either naming them or encapsulating the information more generally in a standard abbreviated formula such as *HFC (heres faciendum curavit,* 'his heir had this erected'). References to heirs are also frequently accompanied by information that the tombstone was erected in accordance with the dead man's will *(heredes exs testamento faciendum curaverunt).* Another common termination used either singly or in combination with one of the other formulae is *HSE* (see above).

Most tombstones follow the pattern set out above but the order in which components appear is variable. An example of funerary inscription analysis is given below, using a soldier's tombstone from Caerleon (*RIB* 365).

Inscription (given line by line in capitals, with component analysis below):

D · M
formal funerary address/

G · VALERIVS · G · F
praenomen / nomen / filiation/

GALERIA · VICTOR
voting tribe / *cognomen /*

LVGDVNI · SIG · LEG · II AVG
origo /   rank /   regiment /

STIP XVII · ANNOR XLV · CV
length of service / age at death / mention

RA · AGENT ANNIO PERPETVO H
of erection of stone by dead man's heir

Latin text (word reconstructions in brackets expand the abbreviations and vertical strokes indicate line endings as shown above on the inscription):

> *D(is) M(anibus) / G(aius) Valerius G(ai) f(ilius) / Galeria (tribu) Victor / Lugduni sig(nifer) leg(ionis) II Aug(ustae) / stip(endiorum) XVII annor(um) XLV cu/ra(m) agent(e) Annio Perpetuo h(erede).*

English translation:
'To the spirits of the departed; Gaius Valerius Victor, son of Gaius, of the Galerian voting tribe, from Lugdunum, standard bearer of the Second Legion Augusta, of seventeen years' service, aged forty-five; set up under the charge of Annius Perpetuus, his heir.'

Although inscriptions do not always adhere to the component order given in the example, with experience it is usually easy to see how translations have been organised. Sometimes certain components are absent from an inscription. Occasionally there is no apparent reason for an omission but it may be quite logical. For example, in Britain the absence of a *cognomen* on a legionary tombstone may indicate a very early date while a missing *praenomen* may suggest a later date as the use of *praenomina* became increasingly rare in the third century. Similarly, the *tria nomina* are uncommon on early auxiliary tombstones as these men were not usually Roman citizens, only being granted the franchise on discharge, and they frequently display just one or two names. Examples of the variety of inscriptions to be found can be seen in the illustrations.

5
Sculptured reliefs on military tombstones

To appraise both the artistic worth and the religious significance of Roman funerary reliefs with reference to even a single province such as Britain is a daunting task. Throughout the Empire stone carvers evolved numerous variations in sculptural style and the influences which affected designs can be seen as clearly on sepulchral monuments as on statuary, public works and religious reliefs. Factors ranging from personal wealth and the level of cultural sophistication to local religious traditions or the presence of a certain army unit could produce results that singled out the funerary art of one area from that of any other. However, the converse is also true; and even more important was the dissemination throughout the Empire of Graeco-Roman techniques and styles, which in some cases blended with local fashions to produce unique forms but more often tended to introduce a uniformity of convention to tombstone design, particularly in the western provinces, where sepulchral traditions were less entrenched than in the east.

The techniques of stone carving which arrived in Britain with the Roman army in AD 43 had already been in use in the Mediterranean world for centuries. Marble, commonly used for funerary monuments in Italy, was not readily available in Britain and limestone was frequently substituted. Otherwise, the techniques and tools used by the Roman sculptor in Britain varied little from contemporary practices in other parts of the Empire. The tools used were chisels of various shapes and sizes, operated in conjunction with a mallet, files and drills. After the stone had been trimmed to the general shape required for the gravestone, claw chisels were used to pick out the rough shape of the figure of the deceased and the niche in which he appeared. The sculptor presumably worked to a drawn plan for figured tombstones although a model was probably required as a basis for high-quality statue production. As the design came nearer to completion finer claw chisels, flat chisels and files were used to form details and create smooth surfaces. Then deep recesses, such as the areas between folds of clothing, were drilled out to give depth to the sculpted relief. Finally, decorative details were completed and the whole front face of the stone, often with the exception of the lower part which was to be buried in the ground, was smoothed firstly with files and then with soft stones or sand. On better preserved tombstones careful observation will reveal a variety of tool marks on the stone and illustrate the techniques used.

On many tombstone reliefs the detail picked out by the stone carver is very impressive (see plates 1 and 2), while on others figures may seem almost naked, being devoid of almost all representations of clothing or equipment (see plate 24). This is because Roman tombstones were originally painted and looked very different from their present appearance. In this way, any details omitted by the sculptor could be added by the artist who painted the tombstone. Indeed, there is evidence in the writings of such classical authors as Pliny, Plutarch, Lucian and Plato to suggest that in the ancient world statue painters, who may on occasion have also painted tomb reliefs, were as highly regarded as sculptors. The colours used for embellishing reliefs included red, blue, yellow, brown, black, white and occasionally green; pink or flesh colour seems to have been used for areas of skin. The finished product, although somewhat gaudy by present-day standards, would probably have seemed most lifelike when new.

The men who introduced classical funerary art into Britain were the stone carvers employed by the invading Roman legions. From this root Romano-British art styles developed, combining Celtic attitudes with imported concepts and designs. However, even in the middle of the first century the work of the legionary sculptors was not of a purely classical form. As the Empire expanded across the Alps, the Romans increasingly became exposed to the Celtic art styles of northern Europe, which, although they remained subordinate to classical concepts, were nevertheless assimilated into the eclectic style typical of Roman military stone carving. The result of this contact between the Mediterranean and barbarian worlds, accelerated by the steady rise in the number of provincial recruits into the Roman army, can be seen in a departure from the pure lines of classical stele design, based on Graeco-Roman architectural prototypes. In its place evolved a series of styles in which the overall traditional idea remained but in an increasingly adulterated form omitting fine detail, a trend which betrays a basic lack of understanding of the individual features of the original design and their importance and function as representations of classical architecture.

An example of this deviation from the original classical tenets can be seen in the presence, on numerous tombstones, of the devolved conch shell or at least its remnant hinge. In Italy, on tombstones which portray a human figure in relief standing within a round-topped niche, a carved conch shell often forms the vault of the niche, with its hinge situated at the apex of the arch. This design was adopted by the Roman army and the conch shell can be clearly seen on the tombstone of an *aquilifer* from Mainz shown in plate 5, where the frilled lower edge of the shell runs behind the man's head. In contrast, on the tombstone of Marcus Favonius Facilis from Colchester (plate 1), the hinge of the conch has devolved to the extent of being no more than a slight dip at the apex of the arch under which the centurion stands. It might be argued that the details of the conch were painted in, but on this tombstone, where so much attention has been paid to other detail, this is unlikely. Clearly, here is an example of a sculptor who adopted conventions from continental works without understanding their purpose.

Although this divergence from purely classical lines, as reflected in military stelae, may seem to be somewhat negative in artistic terms, at the same time the Roman army also evolved certain new styles of its own, suited to its specific needs, which are not found in civilian contexts in Italy. Foremost among these is the series of rider reliefs (plates 14-24), frequently found on cavalry tombstones in the Rhineland and Britain; they had no place in civilian life. The development of specific designs suitable for army requirements is hardly surprising. In the first century AD the legions were often on the move, sometimes being transferred from one end of the Empire to the other, and legionary stone carvers will have had ample opportunity to assimilate styles from several different provinces. In addition, individuals would sometimes be transferred from one legion to another, taking their ideas with them. Even in civilian life some sculptors travelled widely and had far-reaching reputations. Wherever they went, their work will have been copied by local provincial craftsmen. It is also possible that some craftsmen were trained in workshops *(officinae)* in Greece and Italy and then sent out to set up provincial branches elsewhere. In the second and third centuries various centres in the eastern Mediterranean, such as Athens, carried on a flourishing business exporting partially finished marble sarcophagi to other areas such as Gallia Narbonensis in south-east France, where craftsmen in a local *officina* could complete the finer details of relief work and portraits. Undoubtedly, the mechanisms which encouraged the dissemination of sculptural ideas and techniques were persistent and widespread.

In the first half of the first century AD the large military garrison based at several centres along the Rhine in Germany proved an ideal environment for training military sculptors and a fertile breeding ground for new designs for funerary purposes. Consequently, the influences which shaped the ideas behind the design of military stelae in Britain were developed almost entirely from the traditions of the garrison in Germany and are of Rhineland origin. This is to be expected, as the majority of the invasion force of AD 43 had been transferred to Britain from bases in Germany, and the proximity of the mouth of the Rhine to eastern Britain resulted in continuing contact between the two areas throughout the Roman period.

In sculptural technique, form of inscriptions and their use of large figural representations within niches, the better first-century military tombstones from Britain are almost indistinguishable from their Rhineland counterparts. This is especially true of rider relief types, although the Rhineland preference for the inclusion of a *calo*, the soldier's servant, in the background of the scene should not be ignored in such comparisons (see plates 20-1). Another difference between the two areas is the relative scarcity of the funerary banquet scene (plate 12) among examples of sepulchral sculpture from Roman Britain and its common occurrence in Germany. In the one place in Britain where stelae of this type are comparatively common, at Chester, several are associated with civilian burials, and among those primarily the burials of women. These differences apart, the debt owed by funerary art in Britain to Rhineland prototypes is self-evident, albeit in terms of overall style rather than specific detail.

However, a comparison of the tombstones of Genialis from Mainz (plate 7) and Marcus Favonius Facilis from Colchester (plate 1), both of which date to the Julio-Claudian period, may suggest rather more than a transference of style. These two stones have several points of close similarity. In appearance the stance and sculptural execution of the two figures portrayed are very alike and both men stand in an arched niche, the apex of each being formed by a devolved conch-shell hinge. Even more alike are the piers at the sides of the niches; on both stones these are decorated with similar unusual incised motifs, which, in their shallow method of execution, are alien to the nature of raised classical ornament. Both designs take the form of a gently curving incised line which travels from one side of the pier to the other in a zigzag pattern, perhaps meant to represent a spiral fluted column or even scales. On the tombstone of Genialis the pattern terminates in confusion at the top of the piers and this may betray an early attempt at this design of decoration, while the slightly more ornate version on the Colchester stele could represent a later and more developed style. On each stone the funerary inscription occurs immediately below the figural niche, on a flat area without additional carved borders, and both texts are laid out in a similar manner. In addition, both examples are cut in like fashion and the use of the letter 'C' to surround another letter, while not being a rare practice, occurs twice on each inscription. No direct connection between these stones can be established but stylistically the appearance of both is similar enough to suggest that they may have been produced by the same man, a sculptor who worked perhaps firstly in the Mainz area of Germany and then later in Britain, at Colchester, in the wake of the invasion.

Roman tombstones can reveal much more than details of sculptural technique and they provide one of the few sources of information concerning the individual soldier of the period. Inscriptions probably offer the most important statements of fact but the sculptural reliefs often found on military stelae can also render useful data about the deceased. However, it should not be thought that every figure on a tombstone is an exact likeness of the dead man that it commemorates. Distinctive facial character-istics may at first appear to be the basis of unique portraits but in most cases only represent an idealised interpretation of the dead soldier, made to look as formidable and heroic as any warrior yet also as cultured and sophisticated as any Roman. For instance, the face of Marcus Favonius Facilis at first sight appears so individualistic that it might be imagined to be a true likeness of the deceased. But it bears a strong resemblance to a bust, taken to be of the emperor Claudius, found in the river Alde, on which the hair style, broad forehead, jawline and protruding ears can all be paralleled. In the early imperial period the general features of the Julio-Claudian emperors were often copied in this way for busts and grave reliefs, although away from the centre of the Empire sculptors were probably content to offer their clients figures with faces which merely typified the age and station of the deceased.

The representation of clothing and military equipment on figural reliefs appears more accurate than facial features. A stone carver working for the army may not have known the physical characteristics of every dead man for whom he produced a figured tombstone, but he will have been very familiar with the appearance and function of pieces of standard military equipment. The figure of Facilis provides a useful picture of the uniform and equipment worn by a centurion in the middle of the first century. Over his left shoulder and draped across his arm is a cloak, the *sagum,* beneath which he wears a metal cuirass with two rows of leather flaps, presumably some form of kilt, appearing from its lower edge. On his legs he wears greaves and around his waist is a lavishly decorated military belt, the *cingulum,* from which hangs his dagger *(pugio).* On his left side is his sword, slung across his right shoulder on a baldric, and in his right hand he holds his *vitis,* a vine stick, the symbol of office of the centurion. Although the uniform worn by centurions was neither chronologically static nor completely consistent among individuals or different provincial armies, the clothing worn by Facilis is very informative and similar dress is portrayed on the cenotaph of Marcus Caelius (plate 2), erected perhaps forty years earlier in Germany. However, on this stone, Caelius is shown resplendent with full military decorations awarded for service : the circular ornaments, *phalerae,* decorated with the heads of deities and worn on his chest; the two *torques* worn on his shoulders; the thick bracelets, *armillae,* on his wrists; and lastly, on his head, the *corona civica,* the crown of oak leaves awarded for saving the life of a fellow citizen in hazardous circumstances.

Plate 5 provides a good illustration of a legionary eagle *(aquila)* held in the right hand of the *aquilifer* Gnaeus Musius. In his left hand a shield is clearly visible. Another important member of the legion was the *imaginifer* and plate 6 illustrates an imperial *imago* — a portrait of the emperor — in the hands of one named Diogenes, who died at Chester. A better preserved example of an *imago* is that held by Genialis on his tombstone in Mainz (plate 7), where the imperial bust is protected by a canopy.

Roman cavalry tombstones also provide numerous illustrations of both human and horse equipment and the detail expressed in many of the carvings is often as inspired as the flamboyance engendered in the overall scenes of horse and rider in action. Here, not only the representations of the equipment but also the way in which items such as horse harness and saddles were used are important. Several points are obvious on the majority of these stelae: firstly, the absence of stirrups, which were a later invention; secondly, the presence of a much longer sword, the *spatha,* than was used by legionaries; finally, the reliance of the cavalryman on a spear or lance for striking at the enemy.

The use of these two weapons reflects the difference in operational technique between the legionary and the cavalry trooper. The legionary was essentially a heavily armed infantry soldier; in battle he would begin by loosing his two throwing spears *(pila)* at the enemy and then move forward to engage the enemy in vicious close-quarters fighting, in which his short stabbing sword, the *gladius,* would be most effective. For mutual protection the legionaries moved forward as one body, in close order, sheltering behind their shields, and the proximity of one man to another restricted movement and conditioned the technique of calculated stabbing with the *gladius* against enemies whose longer swords were frequently unmanoeuvrable in the melée of battle.

The cavalry were, by contrast, more mobile than the legionaries. Although trained to throw their spears at the enemy, cavalrymen also used them as lances, to impale the enemy while the weapon was still in the rider's hand, as can be observed on the tombstone of Sextus Valerius Genialis from Cirencester (plate 16). Such a tactic would have allowed the rider a much easier contact with an adversary on foot. Likewise, the long *spatha* was essential for reaching the enemy with long sweeping sword strokes, where the *gladius* would have proved too short. The tombstones of Dannicus and Genialis from Cirencester (plates 16 and 18), Rufus Sita from Gloucester (plate 24) and Vonatorix from Bonn (plate 14) illustrate these two weapons. The tombstones of Titus Flavius Bassus from Cologne (plate 21) and Gaius Romanius Capito from Mainz (plate 20) show both weapons and also portray a *calo* in the background, standing ready to give the trooper replacement spears. By contrast, Longinus, on his tombstone at Colchester (plate 15), seems to be lacking in weapons. Why his *spatha* is not shown is a mystery, but certainly his spear would originally have been made of bronze or iron and is no longer present in his damaged right hand. Other tombstones show archers on horseback and the variety of weapons available to the horseman was clearly considerable. Indeed, we know from a commemorative inscription found in North Africa that when the emperor Hadrian reviewed the *cohors VI Commagenorum equitata* in Numidia in AD 128 he complimented the riders of this part-mounted regiment on their ability to hurl stones from slings while on horseback.

Tombstones also depict defensive equipment. The outline of an oval or hexagonal shield can be seen, behind the horse's head, held in the rider's left hand, on most of the cavalry tombstones included here, and those of Vonatorix and Longinus illustrate the wearing of scale-armour cuirasses. Another important item of equipment shown on these stelae is the helmet. The design can be very ornate, as in that worn by Sextus Valerius Genialis (plate 16), or more simple, such as that worn by Rufus Sita (plate 24). It is possible that some of the more grandiose styles portray special cavalry parade helmets worn by the troopers for ceremonial displays. On a very interesting tombstone from Chester (*RIB* 522), a horseman named Aurelius Lucius is shown lying on a couch enjoying a funerary meal, while in the background hangs a very splendid helmet with a large crest and prominent cheek pieces. A similar plumed helmet can be seen worn by Flavinus of the *ala Petriana* (plate 17) on his tombstone, now in Hexham Abbey.

The details of horse equipment shown on these stones are of immense importance to archaeologists as leatherwork has rarely survived and modern reconstructions of Roman horse equipment must rely on contemporary portrayals of horses in harness shown on sculptural panels such as those found on tombstones. More durable were the bronze roundels, also known as *phalerae*, which covered the strap junctions on the harness. These metal discs are sometimes found on Roman fort sites and their purpose is clearly illustrated on plates 14-17 and 20-1. On the tombstone of Longinus (plate 15) the *phalerae* are decorated with rosette motifs and no doubt had a strong ornamental value, as did the small crescent-shaped pendants that can be seen suspended from the harness on the horse ridden by Bassus (plate 22). Such pendants are not infrequently found on fort sites and it is perhaps unusual that they are not represented more often on rider reliefs; it may be that because of their size they were commonly painted rather than sculpted on to the tombstone.

Of fundamental importance to the study of Roman tombstones is an appreciation of the iconography of the stones and the light which it can shed on the philosophy behind Roman sepulchral art and traditions. The interpretation of the images and motifs used on the stelae is particularly interesting when military examples are considered, as it was their task not only to mark the place of interment in the true Roman manner but also to embody the heroic nature of the soldier.

The tombstone was a device closely connected with the concept of *memoria,* being a monument not only to the memory of the dead person, as understood in its modern sense, but also a memorial to the influence, accomplishments and character of the deceased. The proud stance of Marcus Favonius Facilis leaves no doubt as to the kind of man he was and the decorations worn on the chest of Marcus Caelius testify to his bravery, honour and loyal sense of service. Even where no figural representation occurs, such as on the tombstone of Decimus Capienius Urbicus (fig. 4), his position in life, in this instance the rank of *signifer,* is proudly portrayed. Such men can be seen on tombstone after tombstone looking death straight in the face, their achievements in this world and in this life so impressive that they can be sure of victory over death in the next.

In this context, the rider reliefs on early cavalry tombstones again offer an interesting field for investigation. Unlike his legionary counterpart, the *eques* is frequently shown in action. The very pose is intriguing, so divorced is it from the mainstream of Roman funerary art, owing more to large-scale battle scenes shown on certain early imperial monuments. The concept can be seen as typical of the barbarian, non-citizen auxiliary soldiers' attitude towards death, an approach owing little to the citizen interpretation of mortality. In the simplest terms the rider relief can be viewed as an heroic representation of the deceased killing a barbarian foe. This interpretation reveals a basic irony in that the slaughtered foe at the horse's feet represents the barbarian that the cavalryman himself would have been before joining the auxilia — the conversion to a 'them and us' mentality must often have been quite rapid among the unsophisticated auxiliary soldiery. A more sombre explanation might be that the design represents all-conquering death, but this must be considered unlikely in a society with positive expectations of a continuing existence in the afterlife. A more plausible interpretation sees the rider-relief scheme as a symbolic manifestation of the victory of the deceased over death, with the deserving soldier qualifying for happiness in the afterlife while on earth his tombstone acts as a constant reminder of his *memoria* to the living.

In addition to figural representations and inscriptions, tombstones frequently display a variety of other motifs, symbolic of death, mourning and well-being in the afterlife. Common among these are representations of rosettes and stars (plates 2, 8, 10, 11 and fig. 6), which were symbols of prosperity to be enjoyed in the next world and also of apotheosis, the transformation which supposedly took place with the release from earthly life. Continuing in this same vein are the numerous floral motifs, found associated with sepulchral sculpture, often used to decorate the central area of a pediment (fig. 5; plates 9 and 16) or to fill in the spandrels (fig. 3; plates 20-1). In a similar context, the stele shown in plate 4 is of interest. Here, the stone commemorates an *optio* from Chester who died in a shipwreck. Along the bottom of the stone three gable-topped structures are represented; the two outer ones contain shrubs, symbolising life and growth in the next world; the building which they flank, with its stark closed doors, presumably represents a tomb.

Pine cones, such as that seen on the early tombstone of Gaius Mannius Secundus from Wroxeter (plate 11), are another frequently used symbolic device connected with mourning and death, encapsulating the principle of new life springing from the dead seed; the pine cone was closely associated with the ancient fertility goddess Cybele, whose chief sanctuary was in Phrygia in Asia Minor. On this stone the pine cone is flanked by two lions, representing protection for the deceased in his tomb but also symbolising all-devouring death. On the tombstone of Longinus from Colchester two similar lions appear, on either side of a winged sphinx. This creature was a guardian figure but also the enigmatic messenger of divine justice and inescapable death. Representing the mystery of death, the eerie presence of the sphinx can also be observed surmounting the tombstone of Rufus Sita (plate 24), found at Wotton, near Gloucester.

Other commonly used motifs reflect the importance of the belief in a voyage to the Otherworld after death. The conch shell which forms the upper part of the niche on the tombstone of Gnaeus Musius from Mainz symbolises this sea voyage, as do the two sea creatures surmounting the tombstone of Genialis, also at Mainz, and the two dolphins visible to either side of and above the pediment on the tombstone of Sextus Trebonius Proculus (plate 9), who was a member of *Legio XV Apollinaris*, stationed at Carnuntum on the Danube when he died, sometime in the second half of the first century.

Probably, in many cases, the overall symbolic character of the tombstone was the choice of the deceased, either decided upon well in advance or requested in the dead man's last will and testament. To remind the heirs of their duties towards the dead, as laid out in legal documents, soldiers like Genialis, *imaginifer* of *cohors VII Raetorum,* and Caecilius Donatus, a legionary serving at Chester (plate 12), are shown holding scrolls which surely represent their wills. In conclusion, it might be suggested that despite personal religious devotion or the conscientious observance of established rituals by heirs it was the amount of money available which decided how much time should be lavished on the production of a tombstone. The quality of the finished product was, however, related to the skill and imagination of the sculptor.

6
Dating military tombstones

The attribution of a precise calendrical date to a Roman tombstone is usually impossible. A date range relating to a certain emperor's reign is often the best that can be achieved and even this is sometimes not possible. But certain details of tombstone design can be analysed and the evidence can be used to evolve a general set of principles from which criteria for dating can be established in one or more of three ways — historically, stylistically and epigraphically.

There are unfortunately few instances comparable with that of the cenotaph of Marcus Caelius, from the Rhineland, whose death in the *bello Variano* (the Varian war), recorded on the stone (plate 2), gives an unquestionable date, known from other historical sources. However, the movements of many Roman army units, especially those of the legions, are well known. Knowledge of the presence or absence of a particular unit in Britain at a specified time will assist in dating a tombstone commemorating a soldier from that unit. For example, a tombstone relating to *Legio XIV* is unlikely to date after AD 70, the year in which the unit finally left Britain.

Stylistically, several aspects can be useful for dating, notably the style of lettering used, the type of decoration, and fashions depicted in the sculpture. For example, the Emperor Hadrian popularised beards, a style which continued under the Antonine emperors who followed Hadrian in the second century. Before this, a clean-shaven appearance seems to have been preferred and so tombstone reliefs dating to before Hadrian are unlikely to depict men with beards. Types of decoration may be paralleled on several different tombstones, thereby allowing a measure of cross dating. Overall design is also important, as with figured cavalry tombstones, the majority of which date to the first century. Quality of execution of the sculpture on funerary monuments can also be a chronological factor, but caution must be advised here; the tombstone of Longinus (plate 15) from Colchester and those of Sextus Valerius Genialis (plate 16) and Dannicus (plate 18) from Cirencester vary greatly in skill of manufacture, but all were produced before AD 75. However, as a general rule, the quality of lettering on inscribed stelae is usually better in the first century than in the second.

The various formulae used for funerary inscriptions can provide useful indications of date. In Britain the words *Dis Manibus* are found in the early 60s on the tombstone of Julius Classicianus (now in the British Museum), procurator of the province of Britain, the emperor's financial representative in the country. It becomes common in the Flavian period but is abbreviated to *DM* during the second century, although it is still found in its fuller form in the Trajanic period. The absence of this formula usually indicates an early date, before *c* AD 75, especially where the inscription terminates with *h(ic) s(itus) e(st)* (plate 1), a form which regularly occurs on Claudio-Neronian tombstones. More important on first-century inscriptions is the inclusion of the deceased's voting tribe and/or place of origin. The voting tribe designation was soon made redundant, at least in its original form, by the onset of imperial rule and the movement of the frontiers further from Rome. With this expansion a man's *origo,* at first, became much more important, but even this became less significant as time passed and local army recruitment and static garrisons, which became common from the Hadrianic period onwards, led to soldiers originating in the immediate vicinity of the fort where they later served and eventually died.

Increasingly, from the late Republic onwards, the frequent practice of granting Roman citizenship to provincials resulted in a steady growth of the number of people with imperial *gentilicia.* Taking the family name of the emperor (such as Claudius, Flavius, Ulpius or Aurelius) under whom the franchise was awarded seems to have been popular. When this can be observed on tombstone inscriptions, it gives a date before which the deceased could not have received his full Roman name, the *tria nomina.* The existence of a *nomen* adopted from the emperor of the day can only provide an indication, but when assessed with other criteria it can suggest a date within a specific reign. In this method, as in others, correct dating usually relies on the analysis of a combination of features.

7
Museums

A number of museums house either major collections of Roman tombstones or important smaller groups or individual examples worthy of note. In Britain, most well preserved or intrinsically important specimens are on public display. As well as the museums mentioned below, all of which contain military tombstones, several other museums display civilian funerary inscriptions. In addition, there are large collections of Roman military tombstones in museums at Bonn, Cologne and Mainz, West Germany.

Carlisle Museum and Art Gallery, Castle Street, Carlisle, Cumbria CA3 8TP. Telephone: Carlisle (0228) 34781.
Colchester and Essex Museum, The Castle, Colchester, Essex CO1 1TJ. Telephone: Colchester (0206) 76071.
Corinium Museum, Park Street, Cirencester, Gloucestershire GL7 2BX. Telephone: Cirencester (0285) 5611.
Gloucester City Museum and Art Gallery, Brunswick Road, Gloucester GL1 1HP. Telephone: Gloucester (0452) 24131.
Grosvenor Museum, 27 Grosvenor Street, Chester, Cheshire CH1 2DN. Telephone: Chester (0244) 21616 or 313858.
Hexham Abbey, Hexham, Northumberland.
Legionary Museum, Caerleon, Gwent. Telephone: Caerleon (0633) 421462.
Lincoln City and County Museum, Broadgate, Lincoln LN2 1EZ. Telephone: Lincoln (0522) 30401.
Museum of London, London Wall, London EC2Y 5HN. Telephone: 01-600 3699.
Roman Baths Museum, Pump Room, Stall Street, Bath, Avon BA1 2QH. Telephone: Bath (0225) 61111.
Rotherham Museum, Clifton Park, Rotherham, South Yorkshire S65 2AA. Telephone: Rotherham (0709) 2121.
Rowley's House Museum, Barker Street, Shrewsbury, Shropshire. Telephone: Shrewsbury (0743) 61196. Finds from Wroxeter.
South Shields Museum and Art Gallery, Ocean Road, South Shields, Tyne and Wear NE33 2TA. Telephone: South Shields (0632) 568740.
Yorkshire Museum, Museum Gardens, York, North Yorkshire YO1 2DR. Telephone: York (0904) 29745.

8
Further reading

Very little material on Roman tombstones, both civil and military, has been published in English although more literature on the subject exists in German. Consequently, the list of titles below includes several books which devote short but important passages to tombstones within wider discussions concerning either Roman art or social history. Other works dealing specifically with the Roman army or with general epigraphic evidence for Britain are also listed.

Burial and tombstones
Cumont, F. *After Life in Roman Paganism.* 1959.
Liversidge, J. *Britain in the Roman Empire.* 1968. (Pages 464-99.)
Toynbee, J. M. C. *Art in Roman Britain.* 1963.
Toynbee, J. M. C. *Art in Britain under the Romans.* 1964.
Toynbee, J. M. C. *Death and Burial in the Roman World.* 1971.

Roman army
Holder, P. A. *The Auxilia from Augustus to Trajan.* 1980.
Watson, G. R. *The Roman Soldier.* 1969.
Webster, G. *The Roman Imperial Army.* 1969.
Webster, G. *The Roman Army.* Revised edition 1973.

Epigraphic
Birley, A. *The People of Roman Britain.* 1979.
Collingwood, R. G. and Richmond, I. *The Archaeology of Roman Britain.* Revised edition 1969.
Collingwood, R. G. and Wright, R. P. *The Roman Inscriptions of Britain.* 1965. (Inscriptions in this text with an *RIB* number refer to this publication.)
Wright, R. P. and Richmond, I. A. *Catalogue of the Roman Inscribed and Sculptured Stones in the Grosvenor Museum, Chester.* 1955.

Illustrations

In the text accompanying the following illustrations, certain epigraphic conventions have been used; they are as follows: square brackets, [ ], enclose letters which are believed to have been originally engraved but which have been lost through the breaking or defacement of the stone; round brackets, ( ), enclose letters which have been added by an epigrapher to complete an abbreviated word; a stroke, /, indicates a division between lines on the original inscription.

A number of the following inscriptions are accompanied by translations of the Latin text into English. The principal source for most of these translations is Collingwood, R. G. and Wright, R. P., *The Roman Inscriptions of Britain (RIB)*, 1965; however, the readings of a few of the inscriptions have been slightly altered to take account of the findings of more recent epigraphic work, or are the author's translations. All the *RIB* translations are quoted by permission of the Clarendon Press and R. P. Wright and figs. 4-8 are reproduced by their kind permission.

Fig. 1. The provinces of the Roman Empire.

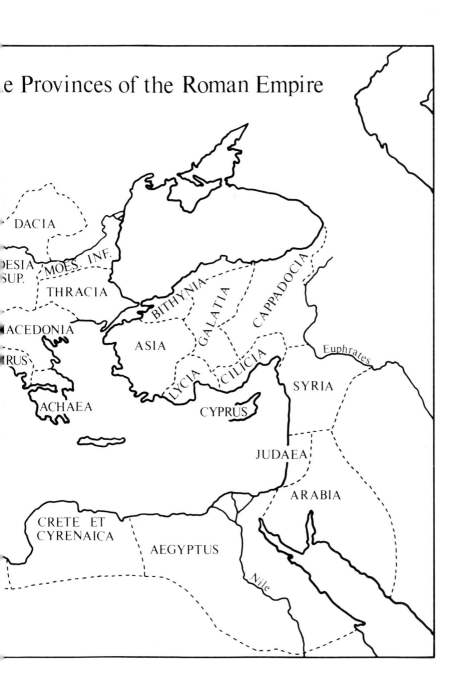

e Provinces of the Roman Empire

DACIA

ESIA
SUP.

MOES. INF.

THRACIA

ACEDONIA

RUS

ASIA

BITHYNIA

GALATIA

CAPPADOCIA

LYCIA

CILICIA

Euphrates

SYRIA

ACHAEA

CYPRUS

JUDAEA

ARABIA

CRETE ET
CYRENAICA

AEGYPTUS

Nile

Fig. 2. Roman Britain: sites mentioned in the text.

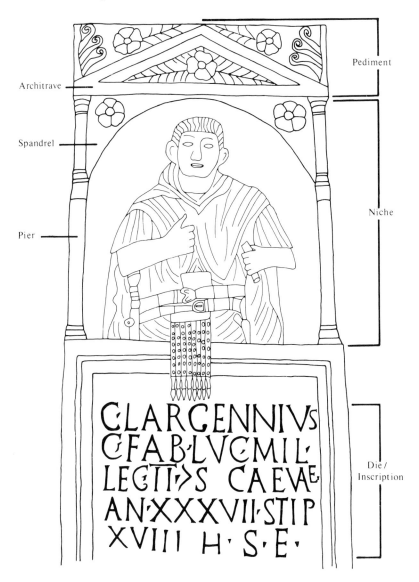

Fig. 3. The component parts of a tombstone. Based on the tombstone of Gaius Largennius, a soldier serving in *Legio II Augusta* at Strasbourg, France. First half of the first century AD. (Drawn by S. Vaughan.)

Plate 1 *(left)*. Tombstone of Marcus Favonius Facilis; Colchester (*RIB* 200). *M(arcus) Favoni(us) M(arci) f(ilius) Pol(lia tribu) Faci/lis c(enturio) leg(ionis) XX; Verecund/us et Novicius lib(erti) posu/erunt; h(ic) s(itus) e(st)*. 'Marcus Favonius Facilis, son of Marcus, of the Pollian voting tribe, centurion of the Twentieth Legion, lies buried here; Verecundus and Novicius, his freedmen, set this up.' Tombstone of Bath oolite, some 1820 millimetres (6 feet) in height. When found in 1868, the stone lay about a metre below the ground surface. Close by, a leaden container holding burnt bones was discovered; presumably the remains of Facilis. (Photograph: copyright Colchester and Essex Museum.)

Plate 2 *(right)*. Cenotaph to Marcus Caelius; Bonn. This stone, found at Xanten on the Rhine, but now in Bonn Museum, shows the legionary centurion Marcus Caelius, son of Titus, who met his death in the Varian disaster of AD 9. It was not until six years after the event that a Roman force visited the site of the catastrophe to bury the dead of three legions in mass graves and so it is certain that the body of Caelius did not lie beneath this stone. Rather than a tombstone, it was a cenotaph, erected to commemorate the dead centurion by his brother Publius Caelius. The two busts which fill the space to either side of the main figure were the dead man's freedmen, who presumably died with him. (Photograph: author.)

Plate 3 *(left).* Tombstone of Caecilius Avitus; Chester (*RIB* 492). This man was an *optio,* the second in command to a centurion. He served with the Twentieth Legion Valeria Victrix; a soldier for fifteen years, he died when he was thirty-four years of age. As can be observed on the last line of the tombstone inscription, *HFC,* an abbreviation of *heres faciendum curavit,* indicates that the stone was erected by the dead man's heir. The tablet case held in Avitus' left hand symbolised his will, written on wax tablets, which no doubt made mention of the provision of a tombstone as a condition of inheritance. (Photograph: copyright Grosvenor Museum, Chester.)

Plate 4 *(right).* Cenotaph to an *optio;* Chester (*RIB* 544). ...]/ *opt[i]onis ad spem / ordinis c(enturia) Lucili / Ingenui, qui / naufragio perit / s(itus) e(st).* '... an *optio,* serving in the century of Lucilius Ingenuus, and awaiting promotion to centurion, who died by shipwreck. He is buried [here].' The nameless subject of this inscription is interesting in that he was an *optio ad spem ordinis,* that is an *optio* who was awaiting promotion to the centurionate, his name presumably having been entered on some form of promotions list. On the last line of the inscription a space was left for the *h(ic)* of the normal *HSE* formula in case the body of this man, lost in a shipwreck, was ever found; apparently it was not. The symbol on the second line, after *ordinis,* is a commonly used abbreviation for either 'century' or 'centurion'. (Photograph: copyright Grosvenor Museum, Chester.)

Plate 5 *(left).* Tombstone of Gnaeus Musius; Mainz. Musius was the *aquilifer* of the Fourteenth Legion Gemina. (Photograph: copyright Mittelrheinisches Landesmuseum, Mainz.)
Plate 6 *(right).* Tombstone of Aurelius Diogenes; Chester (*RIB* 521). Diogenes was the *imaginifer,* probably of the Twentieth Legion Valeria Victrix. The *imago,* held in his right hand, is badly defaced. (Photograph: copyright Grosvenor Museum, Chester.)

Plate 7 *(left)*. Tombstone of Genialis; Mainz. This is a very fine example of the tombstone of an *imaginifer* from an auxiliary regiment, *cohors VII Raetorum,* found at Weisenau. Both inscription and sculptural work are executed in competent style, typical of good craftsmanship of the Rhineland garrison in the middle of the first century. The *imago* held by Genialis probably represents the emperor Claudius. (Photograph: copyright Mittelrheinisches Landesmuseum, Mainz.)

Plate 8 *(right)*. Tombstone of Lucius Duccius Rufinus; York (*RIB* 673). *L(ucius) Duccius / L(uci filius) Volt(inia tribu) Rufi/nus Vien(na) / signif(er) leg(ionis) VIIII / an(norum) XXIIX / h(ic) s(itus) e(st)*. 'Lucius Duccius Rufinus, son of Lucius, of the Voltinian voting tribe, from Vienne, standard bearer of the Ninth Legion, aged 28, lies buried here.' (Photograph: copyright Yorkshire Museum.)

Fig. 4 *(left)*. Tombstone of Decimus Capienius Urbicus; Chester (*RIB* 525). *Dis Manibus* /
D(ecimi) Capieni / *Vrbici Vol/tinia (tribu) Vienn(a)* / *signiferi sti/pend(iorum) XXIIII* /
annor(um) XLIIII / *h(eres) f(aciendum) c(uravit)*. 'To the spirits of the departed (and) of
Decimus Capienius Urbicus, of the Voltinian voting tribe, from Vienna, standard bearer,
of 24 years' service, aged 44. His heir had this erected.'
Fig. 5 *(right)*. Tombstone of Marcus Petronius; Wroxeter (*RIB* 294). *M(arcus) Petronius* /
L(uci) f(ilius) Men(enia tribu) / *Vic(etia) ann(orum)* / *XXXVIII* / *mil(es) leg(ionis)* / *XIIII*
Gem(inae) / *militavit* / *ann(os) XVIII* / *sign(ifer) fuit* / *h(ic) s(itus) e(st)*. 'Marcus Petronius,
son of Lucius, of the Menenian voting tribe, from Vicetia, aged 38, a soldier of the
Fourteenth Legion Gemina, served 18 years, was a standard bearer and lies buried here.'
The absence both of a cognomen for Petronius and of the words *Dis Manibus*, combined
with the formula *hic situs est*, suggests that this is an early tombstone dating to *c* AD 50. In
AD 61 *Legio XIV Gemina* received the additional titles '*Martia Victrix*' and these are also
missing from the inscription.

Plate 9 *(left)*. Tombstone of Sextus Trebonius Proculus; Carnuntum. *Sex(tus) Trebo/nius Q(uinti filius) Fab(ia) / Proculus / Bery(to) corni/cular(ius) leg(ionis) / XV Apol(linaris) stip(endiorum) / XIIII an(norum) XXX / h(ic) [s(itus) e(st)].* 'Sextus Trebonius Proculus, son of Quintus, of the Fabian voting tribe, from Berytus, *cornicularius* of the Fifteenth Legion Apollinaris, of 14 years' service, aged 30, lies buried here.' The *cornicularius* was the senior non-commissioned officer in charge of the staff of clerks in legionary headquarters. (Photograph: author.)

Fig. 6 *(right)*. Tombstone of Gaius Saufeius; Lincoln *(RIB 255)*. *G(aio) Saufeio / G(ai) f(ilio) Fab(ia tribu) Her(aclea) / militi legio(nis) / VIIII / annor(um) XXXX / stip (endiorum) XXII / h(ic) s(itus) e(st).* 'To Gaius Saufeius, son of Gaius, of the Fabian voting tribe, from Heraclea, soldier of the Ninth Legion, aged 40, of 22 years' service; he lies here.'

50

Plate 10 *(left).* Tombstone of Quintus Fortesius Saturninus; Carnuntum. Saturninus served as a common soldier in the Fifteenth Legion Apollinaris; he died sometime in the second half of the first century. (Photograph: author.)

Plate 11 *(right).* Tombstone of Gaius Mannius Secundus; Wroxeter (*RIB* 293). This stone was found in 1752, along with two others (one of which is shown in fig. 5), in the Roman cemetery outside the east gate at Wroxeter. All three are now in Rowley's House Museum, Shrewsbury. This tombstone measures 685 millimetres (27 inches) wide by 1675 millimetres (66 inches) in height but must have stood even taller when positioned in the stone base which was found with it. The penultimate line of the inscription shows that Secundus was a *ben(eficiarius) leg(ati) pr(o praetore)*, a soldier seconded for special duties by the governor of the province. (Photograph: copyright Rowley's House Museum, Shrewsbury.)

Plate 12. Tombstone of Caecilius Donatus; Chester (*RIB* 523). The funerary banquet depicted on this stone shows Donatus reclining on a couch with his wife at his side. The scroll in his left hand probably represents his will while in his right hand he holds a cup. Before him, food for the meal can be seen, placed on a low three-legged table. A third-century date is probable. (Photograph: copyright Grosvenor Museum, Chester.)

Fig. 7. Tombstone of Titus Flavius Candidus; Caerleon (*RIB* 357). *D(is) M(anibus)* / *T(itus) Flavius Candi/dus Vlp(ia) Traiana / m(iles) leg(ionis) II Aug(ustae) / sti(pendiorum)* / *VII an(norum) XXVII / fra(ter) c(uravit).* 'To the spirits of the departed; Titus Flavius Candidus, from Ulpia Trajana, soldier of the Second Legion Augusta, of 7 years' service, aged 27; his brother had this erected.' Candidus' home town of Ulpia Trajana is present-day Xanten on the Rhine, in Germany, yet his tombstone was erected by his brother. It was not uncommon for close relatives to see service in either the same regiment or the same province and such an occurrence best explains this inscription (see plate 2 for a similar fraternal dedication).

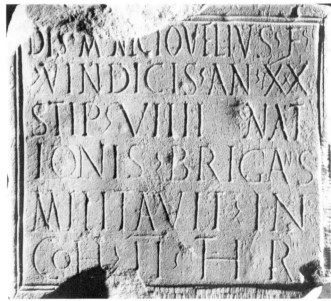

Plate 13. Tombstone of Nectovelius; Mumrills (*RIB* 2142). *Dis M(anibus) Nectovelius f(ilius)* / *Vindicis an(norum) IXXX / stip(endiorum) VIIII nat/ionis Brigans / militavit in / coh(orte) II Thr(acum).* 'To the spirits of the departed: Nectovelius, son of Vindex, aged 29, of 9 years' service, a Brigantian by tribe, served in the Second Cohort of Thracians.' This second-century tombstone from the Antonine Wall in Scotland describes the deceased as belonging to the nation of the Brigantes, a tribe in northern England. It is one of the few sources available which refer to Britons serving in the Roman Army, but, as in other provinces, by the second century many recruits must have been of local origin. (Photograph: copyright National Museum of Antiquities of Scotland, Edinburgh.)

Plate 14. Tombstone of Vonatorix; Bonn. *Vonatorix Du/conis f(ilius) eques ala /
Longiniana an/norum XLV stipen/diorum XVII h(ic) s(itus) e(st).* 'Vonatorix, son of
Duco, trooper from the cavalry regiment Longiniana, aged 45, of 17 years' service, lies
buried here.' This tombstone dates to the middle of the first century and is typical of a
group of several early cavalry stelae produced at Bonn, which show only a rider on a
springing horse. This series was followed, at a slightly later date (before AD 70), by the
more familiar type of tombstone showing a cavalryman riding down a barbarian.
(Photograph: author.)

Plate 15. Tombstone of Longinus; Colchester (*RIB* 201). *Longinus Sdapeze | Matygi f(ilius) duplicarius | ala prima Tracum pago | Sardi(ca) anno(rum) XL aeror(um) XV | heredes exs testam(ento) [f(aciendum)] c(uraverunt) | h(ic) s(itus) e(st).* 'Longinus Sdapeze, son of Matycus, *duplicarius* from the first cavalry regiment of Thracians, from the district of Sardica, aged 40, of 15 years' service, lies buried here; his heirs under his will had this set up.' Longinus Sdapeze came from Sardica, the modern Sofia. (Photograph: copyright Colchester and Essex Museum.)

Plate 16. Tombstone of Sextus Valerius Genialis; Cirencester (*RIB* 109). Sextus Valerius Genialis was a trooper of the cavalry regiment of Thracians, a Frisian tribesman, who served in the *turma* (troop) of Genialis. His tombstone, set up by his heir, dates most probably to the Neronian period, when the *ala prima Thracum* had been transferred to Cirencester, perhaps from Colchester, where its presence is demonstrated by the stele of Longinus (plate 15). (Photograph: copyright Corinium Museum, Cirencester.)

Plate 17 *(left).* Tombstone of Flavinus; Hexham Abbey (*RIB* 1172). *Dis Manibus Flavinus / eq(ues) alae Petr(ianae) signifer / tur(ma) Candidi an(norum) XXV / stip(endiorum) VII h(ic) s(itus) e(st).* 'To the spirits of the departed: Flavinus, trooper of the cavalry squadron Petriana, standard bearer, from the troop of Candidus, aged 25, of 7 years' service, lies buried here.' This stone was discovered in 1881 in the foundations of the porch outside the south transept of Hexham Abbey but presumably originated at the nearby Roman fort site of Corbridge. Flavinus is portrayed wearing a plumed helmet and in his right hand holds a staff topped by what appears to be an *imago*. It is, therefore, peculiar that he is described as a *signifer* rather than an *imaginifer*. (Photograph: copyright Hexham Abbey.)
Plate 18 *(right).* Tombstone of Dannicus; Cirencester (*RIB* 108). *Dannicus eq(u)es alae / Indian(ae) tur(ma) Albani / stip(endiorum) XVI cives Raur(icus) / cur(averunt) Fulvius Natalis it / Fl[av]ius Bitucus ex testame(nto) / h(ic) s(itus) e(st).* 'Dannicus, trooper of the cavalry regiment Indiana, from the troop of Albanus, of 16 years' service, a tribesman of the Raurici, lies buried here. Fulvius Natalis and Flavius Bitucus had this erected under his will.' The Raurici were a tribe based in the vicinity of the Roman colony of Augusta Raurica, the modern Augst, near Basle in Switzerland. (Photograph: copyright Corinium Museum, Cirencester.)

Plate 19. Tombstone of Lucius Vitellius Tancinus; Bath (*RIB* 159). Tancinus was a tribesman of Caurium, in Spain, who served in the cavalry regiment of Vettones, a unit raised in Spain. The stone is typical of cavalry stelae of the first century and has much in common with those of the Claudio-Neronian period. However, on the inscription the regimental name carries the suffix *cR* for *civium Romanorum* (meaning 'Roman citizens'), an honorific title not awarded to units before the Flavian period. This stone is therefore probably of Vespasianic date, *c* AD 74. (Photograph: copyright Roman Baths Museum, Bath.)

Fig. 8 *(left)*. Tombstone of Candidus; Brecon Gaer (*RIB* 403).*Diis M[anibus] / Cand[idi....]/ni fili [eq(uitis) alae] /Hisp(anorum) Vett(onum) [c(ivium) R(omanorum) tur(ma)] / Clem(entis) dom[o ....] / an(norum) XX stip(endiorum) III H[...* 'To the spirits of the departed (and) of Candidus, son of [....]nus, trooper of the cavalry regiment of Vettonian Spaniards, Roman citizens, of the troop of Clemens, from ....; aged 20, of 3 years' service; ....' The text given above is a probable reconstruction of this fragmentary inscription. Candidus, as a trooper of the *ala Vettonum,* was a member of the same regiment as Lucius Vitellius Tancinus (see plate 19), but this tombstone is later in date than the example from Bath and the findspot represents a posting subsequent to the unit's stay in the south-west of England, perhaps *c* AD 75 when the Governor of Britain, Sextus Julius Frontinus, reasserted Roman control over most parts of Wales.

Plate 20 *(right).* Tombstone of Gaius Romanius Capito; Mainz. This stele is one of the best preserved and executed examples of funerary sculpture in the Mainz area. It portrays Gaius Romanius Capito, a trooper of the cavalry regiment of Noricans, riding down a barbarian while his servant stands in the background holding replacement weapons. Neronian in date. (Photograph: author.)

Plate 21. Tombstone of Titus Flavius Bassus; Cologne. Like Gaius Romanius Capito (plate 20), Bassus was also a trooper in the *ala Noricorum,* and his funerary relief is of similar style. The stone dates to the late first century and represents a later posting of the regiment, from Mainz to Cologne. (Photograph: author.)

Plate 22. Detail of the tombstone of Bassus; Cologne. This plate shows a detail of the
horse and rider from the tombstone of Titus Flavius Bassus, shown in full on plate 21.
Cavalry tombstones frequently portray items of horse equipment, in particular leather
straps and the circular *phalerae* which decorate the harness; however, this stele also shows
examples of the highly decorated pendants which hung from the strapwork on Roman
cavalrymen's horses. On this picture, such pendants can be seen just above the horse's
right front leg and on a strap hanging from its mane. (Photograph: author.)

Plate 23 *(opposite).* Tombstone of Tiberius Claudius Tirintius; Wroxeter (*RIB* 291).
*Tib(erius) Claud(ius) Tiri/ntius eq(ues) coh(ortis) [..] / Thracum an[n] / orum LVII
sti[p]/endior(um) XX [...] / h(ic) s(itus) [e(st)].* 'Tiberius Claudius Tirintius, trooper of the
.... cohort of Thracians, aged 57, of ..... years' service, lies here.' Although his
tombstone was based on the design of those favoured by cavalrymen in *alae*, Tirintius
enjoyed less status and pay than soldiers in cavalry regiments for he was only a trooper in a
cohors equitata, a part-mounted unit. (Photograph: copyright Rowley's House Museum,
Shrewsbury.)

Plate 24. Tombstone of Rufus Sita; Gloucester (*RIB* 121).*Rufus Sita eques c(o)ho(rtis) VI /
Tracum ann(orum) XL stip(endiorum) XXII / heredes exs test(amento) f(aciendum)
curave(runt) / h(ic) s(itus) e(st).* 'Rufus Sita, trooper of the sixth cohort of Thracians, aged
40, of 22 years' service, lies buried here. His heirs had this erected according to the terms
of his will.' The tombstone of Rufus Sita illustrates that, despite having a lower financial
and military status than their cavalry counterparts, horsemen in part-mounted cohorts,
such as the *VI Thracum,* could still afford lavish funerary monuments, at least on occasion.
(Photograph: copyright Gloucester City Museum.)

63

Index

Page numbers in italic refer to illustrations.